Spinosaurus

by Grace Hansen

WITHDRAWN

Abdo
DINOSAURS
Kids

abdopublishing.com

Published by Abdo Kids, a division of ABDO, P.O. Box 398166, Minneapolis, Minnesota 55439.

Copyright © 2018 by Abdo Consulting Group, Inc. International copyrights reserved in all countries.
No part of this book may be reproduced in any form without written permission from the publisher.

Printed in the United States of America, North Mankato, Minnesota.

052017

092017

 THIS BOOK CONTAINS
RECYCLED MATERIALS

Photo Credits: Alamy, AP Images, iStock, Science Source, Shutterstock, Thinkstock,
©Bramfab p.13,21 / CC-BY-SA-4.0, ©Ghedoghedo p.21 / CC-BY-SA-4.0

Production Contributors: Teddy Borth, Jennie Forsberg, Grace Hansen

Design Contributors: Dorothy Toth, Laura Mitchell

Publisher's Cataloging in Publication Data

Names: Hansen, Grace, author.

Title: Spinosaurus / by Grace Hansen.

Description: Minneapolis, Minnesota : Abdo Kids, 2018 | Series: Dinosaurs |
    Includes bibliographical references and index.

Identifiers: LCCN 2016962384 | ISBN 9781532100390 (lib. bdg.) |
    ISBN 9781532101083 (ebook) | ISBN 9781532101632 (Read-to-me ebook)

Subjects: LCSH: Spinosaurus--Juvenile literature. | Dinosaurs--North America--
    Juvenile literature.

Classification: DDC 567.912--dc23

LC record available at http://lccn.loc.gov/2016962384

Table of Contents

Spinosaurus

Spinosaurus lived in the **Cretaceous period**. That was about 95 million years ago.

Spinosaurus was a **theropod**.

It ate meat.

Body

Spinosaurus was the largest meat-eating dinosaur. It grew more than 50 feet (15.24 m) long! It could weigh more than 16,000 pounds (7,257.5 kg).

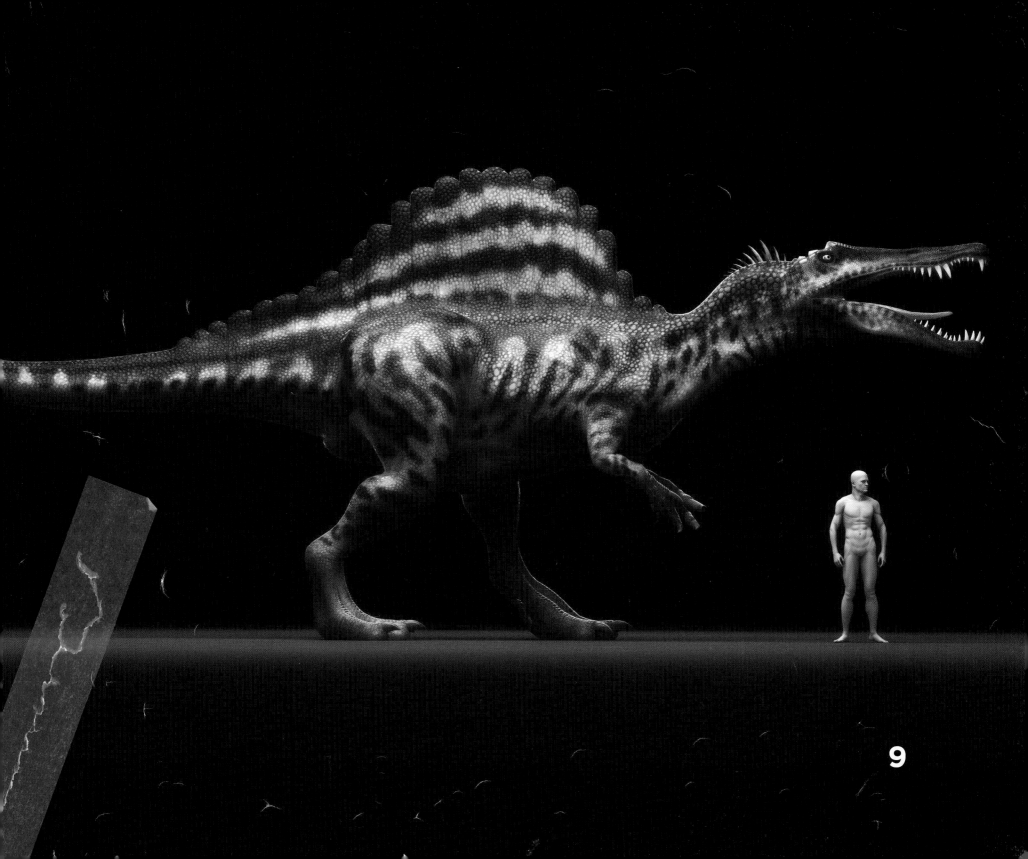

Spinosaurus is well known for the large sail on its back. The sail was made up of spines. The spines were connected by skin.

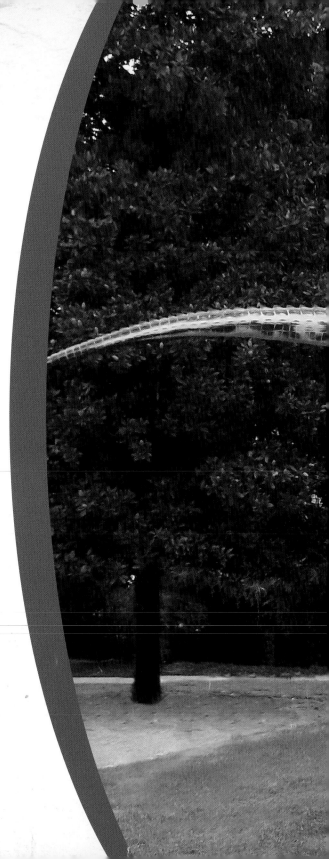

Spinosaurus had short arms. It had strong legs with clawed feet. Its long tail made up about half of its length.

Spinosaurus had a long snout and mouth. It looked like a crocodile's mouth. It also had lots of long, pointed teeth.

Habitat & Food

Spinosaurus spent time in water and on land. But it probably moved much easier in water. It ate lots of large fish. It even ate sharks!

Fossils

Spinosaurus **fossils** have been found in northern Africa. This area was filled with many bodies of water in the **Cretaceous period**. Today it is a large desert called the Sahara.

The first **fossils** were uncovered in Egypt in 1912. In 2008, a piece of finger bone and spine were found in Morocco.

Morocco

Egypt

More Facts

- The museum that held the most complete Spinosaurus remains was bombed in World War II. The **fossils** were destroyed.

- Spinosaurus had a **snout** filled with widely-spaced teeth. This was great for catching fish and other food.

- A Spinosaurus head was shaped much like a crocodile's. However, it was much larger at around 5 to 6 feet (1.5 to 1.8 m) long.

Glossary

Cretaceous period – rocks from the Cretaceous period often show early insects and the first flowering plants. The end of the Cretaceous period, about 65 million years ago, brought the mass extinction of dinosaurs.

fossil – the remains, impression, or trace of something that lived long ago, as a skeleton, footprint, etc.

sail – a broad, upright, and elongated spine that some dinosaurs had. It was likely used to control the body temperature of the dinosaur.

snout – the projecting nose and mouth of an animal.

theropod – a meat-eating dinosaur that came in many sizes and usually had small forelimbs.

Index

abdokids.com

Use this code to log on to abdokids.com and access crafts, games, videos and more!

Abdo Kids Code:
DSK0390